1 Navvy shanty and child labour, Manchester Ship Canal *c.* 1890.

2 *Overleaf* Matriarchal tradition in full. The whip was for the horse . . . but the husbands obeyed. Although clearly a mock-up – the background of a rough sea is hardly apposite – the 'uniform' was both typical and genuine.

Victorian and Edwardian

CANALS

from old photographs

Introduction and commentaries by

D. D. GLADWIN

PORTMAN BOOKS

LONDON

First published 1976
Reprinted 1983
This edition published 1989 by
Portman Books, an imprint of
B.T. Batsford Ltd
4 Fitzhardinge Street, London W1H 0AH
Text copyright © D. D. Gladwin, 1976

ISBN 0 7134 3061 3

Printed and bound in Great Britain by
Courier International Ltd
Tiptree, Essex

3 The tranquillity of a pre-war river. The Thames at Molesey Lock. The patriarchal lock-keeper is, we trust, reading his Rules and Regulations.

Contents

4 Child labour was still legal when this photograph of the navvies on the Manchester Ship Canal was taken in 1889.

Acknowledgments

Photograph 27 is reproduced by gracious permission of H.M. the Queen. L. A. Edwards lent 60, 137, 138, 149, 159, 160 and Mr. L. D. Elder 109. Nos. 126, 145, 165–7 are from the Peter L. Smith Collection and 11 is from Ramsey and Muspratt, Cambridge. The Museum of English Country Life at the University of Reading lent nos. 12, 28, 39, 120, 156 as well as 29–31 and 133 (Miss C. Bushell). A number of the photographs are reproduced by courtesy of Public Libraries; Manchester Public Libraries 1, 4, 37, 56, 113, 122, 164; Birmingham Public Libraries 40, 46, 115–16, 121, 124, 140; Hull Public Libraries 68; Dartford Library 97; Richmond Public Library 139; Oxford City Library 38, 66, 151, 163; York Public Library 41; Bury St Edmunds Public Library 118 and Leeds Public Library 142. 114 is from the West Suffolk Record Office, 92 from the Bodleian Library Oxford. Nos. 47, 132 and 152 are from the National Monuments Record, no. 43 from the Science Museum. No. 154 is from the Museum of British Transport; 146 is from the Welsh Folk Museum, St Fagans, Cardiff. No. 34 is from Hugh McKnight, nos. 7, 127, 143 from the G. W. Wilson Collection, Aberdeen University Library. 3 and 147 are from the Radio Times Hulton Picture Library.

Apart from the collections of the Author and the Publisher the principal source has been the museum of the British Waterways Board at Stoke Bruerne. The help of Mr. R. J. Hutchings, the curator is gratefully acknowledged together with the provision of nos. 2, 11, 16, 32, 36, 50, 55, 61–5, 67, 70–2, 75, 81, 85–6, 88, 98–100, 104, 106, 150, 158.

5 Perhaps the best known lock on the Thames, Boulters, but for once showing the man who ran it, and the equipment.

Introduction

The making of navigable waterways in Britain was started by the Romans with the Caer and Foss Dykes and lasted until the opening of the Manchester Ship Canal in 1894. The expansion period of water transport was from the navigable rivers of, roughly, 1700 until the opening of the Birmingham and Liverpool Junction Canal in 1835; by 1840 railways had taken over the bulk of the traffic. Some canals were assimilated and used to good effect, others were brought up and put to death, while yet another part of the system was left to wither away and die.

Not all died though, and after some reorganisation and acceptance of the fact that they had to fight back, some independents did fight and to such an extent that the shareholders, the boatmen and the maintenance men all made a living, albeit on a diminished scale. In the case of the narrow canals, the boatman took his family on board – giving the company two, three or four persons' work for the wage of one – and used the boat as his home. On the wide canals new traffics were found or old ones regained with, rather oddly, the canal being able to give a quicker delivery, waterside to waterside, than the railways. To some degree this position was exacerbated by the railways strangling themselves with traffic. Some of the railway-owned canals were used in a fratricidal war against other railways; not having rail access to a given patch but having shrewdly bought up a canal thereabouts what better than to use it as a feeder? In one specific case, the Birmingham Canal Navigations, leased to the LNWR, was made profitable for the railway by using the network for short-haul, heavy tonnage, quick turnaround traffic: coal and iron. This dismemberment of the system betwixt rail and independent interests made through-carrying difficult but, despite often punitive tolls, canal and river carrying had, if not a golden, at least a silver age between 1860 and the outbreak of war in 1914. Typical tonnages handled in one year (1905) were the Staffordshire & Worcestershire Canal at 722,000, the Trent & Mersey Canal at over 1,000,000 and the Birmingham Canal Navigations no less than 7,546,453.

A problem that arose when compiling this book was the dearth of photographs depicting industrial scenes. With the cooperation of W. K. V. Gale, the ironmaster, we looked through one of the largest collections of photographs showing ironworks, the majority of those in Wales and the Midlands being situated alongside canals by which coal, ore and flux were brought in and the finished products easily taken out. Although many illustrations were taken across the canal, or from a canal bridge, the actual course of the waterway was omitted. Similarly, while it was not too difficult to find 'gaggles' of narrow boats engaged on long hauls, and wherries and the like, the too often unkempt 'joey' (day) coal-boats in the Midlands proved very shy. The reason, naturally enough, is simply that they were not attractive or 'quaint'; neither were any of the owners inspired to have publicity photographs taken.

Unavoidably any collection like this has to be unbalanced – in strict proportion I suppose the ratio of commercial to pleasure boats, with the exception of the Thames, would be of the order of 250:1, but to utilise this ratio would make the book boringly repetitive. Therefore I have included as much variety as possible. Similarly, it has to be that some waterways are omitted: even today Edwards's *vade mecum** lists 114 separate navigations, while on the Grand Junction Canal which, because of its length, variety and proximity to the 'Great Wen', always caught the photographer's eye, more than one view is shown.

The Thames has always been the odd one out, the lock-keepers were smart, the locks well kept and as long ago as 1866 orders were issued 'that notices for the sale of refreshments be not exhibited at the premises of the lock-keepers' while contemporaneously the rates for pleasure craft were fixed. Such amenities were unthinkable on the strictly commercial canals. In 1897 so unbalanced had the thinking of the Thames Conservancy become that at Richmond and Teddington locks passenger steamers plying to Molesey be given precedence over the barge traffic; at the other locks the passenger and barge traffic be passed by alternate lockages; and at Teddington on Saturdays, Sundays, and all public holidays priority be given generally to all

* L.A. Edwards, *Inland Waterways of Great Britain*, 1972.

pleasure traffic over the barges'. Therefore of commercial traffic on the Thames I can offer little; but of pleasure much.

Such heresies must have set the old barge-masters rotating in their graves!

Seriously, it has to be admitted that canal people have for a long time been regarded as pariahs, probably as an atavistic hangover from the days of 'navigators' – those sturdy men who hacked, dug, blasted, cursed and died digging out our water channels. When the Manchester Ship Canal was being dug they had mechanical aids (10 dredgers, 97 steam excavators and 230 miles of railway) but for all this they were basically 'those magnificent men'.

Boatmen were, and until the last one is laid in Braunston Churchyard, still are, an independent race of men and women – whether 'Water Gypsies' in the Midlands, 'Turnpike Sailors' in my own East Anglia, 'Kenspeckle' on the Forth & Clyde or 'Boolies' on the Humber. When they took to living on boats, as perforce they had to – it is claimed that Thomas Monk, a carrier from Tipton, started the process in 1825 – they took with them all the virtues of the peasant, the folklore of generations and the independence of a squire.

That conditions in the cabins of boats, especially the relatively cramped 'monkey' or 'narrow' boats that plied from Manchester to Birmingham, Birmingham to London, London to Leicester, to Nottingham, to Chesterfield 'and to all places adjacent thereto' as the old advertisements have it, were rough by our standards is undeniable. George Smith, the mid-nineteenth-century 'do-gooder' had his own axe to grind when he claimed the boat cabins were 'hell-holes . . . they eat together, sleep together, drink together, live together and die together in these filthy places' but another writer almost his contemporary, H. R. Robertson, gives us, in his *Life on the Upper Thames*, another less rabid viewpoint: 'The spotless neatness of the little cabin, and the last polish bestowed on the brass fittings are characteristics . . . The exterior decoration of these boats is noticeable, and evinces the pride taken in their appearance . . .' It has been claimed, with some justice, that boatmen and their families were illiterate; true, but then so were over 30% of the working population; that boatmen liked a drop of liquor – true, but fresh water was hard to come by, furthermore steering a boat dead drunk did not mean that anyone got hurt, whereas today we need breathalysers; that boatmen were unhygienic but then look how the people on the bank lived – 'With broken panes in every window-frame, and filth and vermin in every nook. With the walls unwhitewashed for years, black with the smoke of foul chimneys, without water, and corded bed-stocks for beds, and sacking for bed clothing, with floors unwashed from year to year, without offices . . .'

Instead of accepting written evidence, let us look at what the photographs tell us. As a boatman long since beyond caring told me: 'We wore white corduroy trousers, with bell bottoms, and the velvet seams and the diamond stitching, fancy knitted braces with brass buckles, and used to have the silk thrums what we used to use in the whip to go across from buckle to buckle, tied in a bow down the front and a white cotton hand-made shirt with feathered stitching all down the front and the boots were polished like glass before you started the day'; and the women, well! they were smart, as you can see.

The canal itself has been vilified to such an extent that the subject becomes boring; it was blamed for cholera in 1815, called 'noisome' and 'a dreary waste of cinders and watery lines'. If we accept this as true, why did people go for boat trips? Accepting it as true why didn't the children of the age drop dead after swimming? Accepting it as true why did the people go for strolls along the towpath? Simply the answer is that for every mile of factories, there were fifty of countryside; for every mile of dirt, there were fifty of clean, and for every mile of stagnant water, fifty were moving – however imperceptibly. One of the hoariest tales about canals is that they are flat. Statistically there is one lock every 1.37 miles, and every time a boat goes through the lock it uses (according to size) 25,000–70,000 gallons of water taken from one level and passed down to another. The canal is fed by drainage from roads, from streams, from springs, from rivers and from rainfall; in turn the overflow goes over the weirs, over the locks, and to some degree is abstracted by factories – even, would you believe, some to the waterworks. Finally, every engineer worth his salt would build his canal to give a flow of 'one-half of one mile per hour'.

Canal architecture, both in the construction of locks and their appurtenances, cuttings and embankments, lock houses, stables, aqueducts and bridges, was and is unique. Largely unassuming, the elegant brick bridge at Stoke Bruerne, the staithes at York, the lockhouse at Caversham, the pub on Hickling Broad, all of these were built by men with an eye to the fitting; built of the indigenous stone or brick, of a wood that weathers to a silver grey and with a grace and charm that we, somewhere, have lost.

No attempt has been made to correlate the scenes of the period and today; thirty years ago this might have been possible, but with today's ever increasing rate of rebuilding and 'erasure' (the official word) of canalside structures, both by officialdom in the guise of environmental improvements and by the amenity industry, comparison becomes meaningless. The immense variety of craft are swept away, sailing and horse-drawn barges first, then narrow boats, while on the thriving waterways of the North East modernisation takes its toll of older boats. Instead of charm we have functionalism. So be it, if this is progress; but a little nostalgia never did harm!

PEOPLE

6 'Poor paddy works on the railway' or in this case, the Manchester Ship Canal. Navvies yes – but white shirts?

7   The fine body of Scottish gentlemen are on board their tug, probably on the Forth and Clyde Canal;
c. 1880.

8   The 'quant' or shaft is ominously to the fore in this view of the Eastern Counties Navigation and
Transport Company's directors inspecting the works of the River Lark shortly after their takeover in 1889.

9 Grand Junction Canal at Braunston. This photograph depicts, we hope, two families, as the cabins would otherwise be grossly over-crowded. A curious discrepancy is that while the children on the bank are fully dressed, the two on the boat have uncovered heads, a sight rarely seen on boats even in fairly recent times; the boy has borrowed Dad's flat 'at!

10 A rather sentimental and contrived picture, originally titled 'Having tea in a monkey boat cabin', which indicates authentic components of a standard narrow boat back cabin.

11 River Cam, Jesus Locks, 1887. The Conservators, wearing a variety of headgear, are about to leave on their annual pilgrimage. The curved lock gate balance beams to the left are pleasing to the eye.

12 The Boss. George Casebourne, Resident Engineer of the Bude Canal, about 1860. Not an easy canal to manage and far from profitable, it served to bring sea-sand to neighbouring farmers as manure.

Next page **13–18** Canal visionaries of the late Victorian era: officials of the Manchester Ship Canal including from top to bottom and left to right: J. K. Bythell, Chairman; Earl Egerton of Tatton, Chairman 1887–94; Sir E. Leader Williams, Designer and Engineer-in-Chief; Marshall Stevens, First Manager; Sheriff Lawrence, M.P., Member of the Provisional Committee; Daniel Adamson, Chairman of Provisional Committee and first Chairman.

19 Posed – no horse, no mast. The upturned tiller is in the 'at rest' position. The photograph has been retouched, though this is as it was first published in 1903; the dog, surely, has been painted in – the poor brute would be burnt on the chimney. And a cup and saucer? The mind boggles! But it does show the clothing actually worn.

20 The process of legging served to work an unmotorized boat through tunnels before the introduction of steam tugs and motor boats. Maida Hill tunnel, Regents Canal.

21 *Left* Narrow boats in London, 1903. '. . . and presently you hap on youngsters engaged in the delicate operations of the toilet in full view of all the world that cares to look'.

22 *Below* A courting couple.

23 Variety of craft in Birmingham about 1911. The long distance boats of Fellows, Morton & Clayton contrast with the collieries boat of T & W Griffiths. 'Traditional décor' is well evidenced, while the horse's tail attached to the helm of *Walnut* (as with many other narrow boats) is clearly depicted. This tail was often that of a favourite horse which had died, the belief being that the strength, stamina and speed of the animal were then conferred on the boat. The clothing is almost a uniform, including the leather belt (to carry a windlass) of the younger woman. The child is exquisitely dressed as a replica of her mother; the necklace would not be worn in working conditions for fear of accidents. Many canal girls were (and are) pretty by reason of their healthy complexions, although the men did not wear so well.

24 Steamer captains and crew were in their time the élite of canalmen. Their pride in appearance of both themselves and their boat is obvious.

25 Not one of the best dressed crews, but rather more typical. Berkhamsted, Grand Junction Canal, around 1900.

26 River Medina, Isle of Wight, near Newport. These craft were used often enough on the Portsmouth and Arundel Canal. On the timber barge the crew (all one of him!) is easing the steering by means of a quant.

BOATS

27   Improbable but true. An experimental steam 3-ton launch, the *Ichthyon*, designed by Captain Beadan, R.N.; photographed in 1858.

28–31   Bushell Brothers Boatyard at Tring, Grand Junction Canal in 1892.

28   *Right* Wielding an adze.

29   *Opposite, top to bottom* Both pleasure and commercial boats are on the stocks. The variety in coal types on the wharf bears witness to their other activity.

30   Painting one and building another, a sign of flourishing trade. The 'hoe' (left foreground) is used to fish lost or mislaid items out of the canal.

31   60-ton barge newly launched in 1902. The men had reason to be proud of their work.

32 *Above* The steamer *Delamare* complete with collapsible funnel, on the River Weaver, *c.* 1884.

33 *Left* Fellows, Morton and Clayton steamer and butty on the Grand Junction Canal at Boxmoor. The method of controlling the towrope from the cabin's top via running blocks is apparent.

34 *Below* The steam tug *Buffalo* about 1906 on the Grand Junction Canal. The enormous funnel and headlight typify this class of craft.

35 Trailing clouds of steam and glory the pride of Fellows, Morton and Clayton makes its way along the Grand Junction Canal; *c.* 1902.

36 The horses are brought over the hill at Braunston and have a meal while waiting for the tug to bring the boats.

37 A new narrow boat, *Reggie*, for Albert Wood, canal carriers of Manchester, is ready for launching into the Rochdale Canal at Sowerby Bridge.

38 The smart and well painted *Fanny*, near Hythe Bridge, Oxford Canal, about 1890. Note that neither brass bands nor chains are visible on the chimney.

39 Bude Canal 1860. A steam launch arriving for lunch.

40 Stratford-on-Avon Canal at Lapworth. Aside from the two boat-children, who are certainly
well-dressed, the planks and stands on this boat differ quite considerably from those on, say, the
Grand Junction Canal.

41 The masts have not been shot away by the cannon, but were always lowered to 'shoot' bridges.
River Ouse, York, around 1880.

42 River Brue, Belaugh, 1902. By the nature of its design a wherry could not always sail round corners, though a couple of quants could persuade it to point the right way!

43 Old, but not as old as its navigation, is York. The keel on the left must have been antiquated even in 1845, when Fox Talbot took this photograph, while the blocks of the right-hand craft would serve a man-o'-war, let alone a 40-tonner.

44   Thames, Sonning Lock, 1890: note the wooden lock fendering.

45   Stoke Bruerne, Grand Junction Canal, in the 1890s. The fore-cabin served to accommodate any family exceeding the three allowed in the back cabin.

46   Leeds, March 1910.

48   *Right, above* Presumably after stabling the horse, bow-hauling in the River Wey at its junction with the Basingstoke Canal.

47   A smart pair working up the Grand Junction Canal. Unusual to see shafting in progress – also the mast.

49   *Right* Outside Islington Tunnel 1910. The downturned tillers indicate they are waiting, probably for the tug.

50 Mélange at Braunston Tunnel. Horseboats, steam tug, pleasure craft. The horse is using his nose-tin, the girl looks hungry.

51 Grand Junction Canal near Weedon, 1906. The boats have been allowed, for photographic purposes, to overtake the horse.

52　Gas-oil boats of Thomas Clayton (Oldbury) around the turn of the century. The lead horse was probably both a biter and very nervous. It was not uncommon for hunters, dray- and tram-horses to be used, especially for railway (as opposed to privately) owned boats. In the former case each animal had both name and number, but it was a matter of 'pot-luck' which man and horse combination occured.

53　Meaford, near Stone, Trent & Mersey Canal.

54 Chiswick Eyot, Thames, December 1909. The *Five Sisters* was built at Chiswick in the 1870s, albeit registered in Rochester. One man and a boy would take a barge similar to this to Faversham, Upnor, Sittingbourne, Southend or 'East Coast-wise' even as far as Newcastle or the Isle of Wight. Loads varied from 10 tons – the *Two Sisters* – to 140 tons – the *Edith* – carrying manures, ashes, coke, coal, bricks, cement, flint or corn. Degraded, they could have a load of 'rough stuff' (rubbish) shot in and shovelled out(!) or, short of freight, they might go oyster and sprat fishing.

56 A steam navvy of the 1880s in use on the Manchester Ship Canal.

55 *Below* A magnificent steam bucket dredger of 1892. Operated by T. Laver & Co., the *Empress* could shift 100 tons of mud an hour.

57 Yarmouth, from Breydon Water, 1900. The wherry, running light, has a single reef (or tuck) in and is just maintaining steerage way. The boat on the right was the local ferry.

58 *Left, above* A wherry going 'full chat' near Horning 1902. Now inundated with pleasure craft, in those halcyon days only a dinghy ties up at the staithe!

59 *Left* One of the last commercial craft on the Arun Navigation: Henry Doick, bargemaster, near Pulborough, *c.* 1885.

60 *Above* An outstanding example of a Humber keel seen on the Welland at Spalding in 1900.

61 Coke forks, picks, shovels (both pan and digging) have been called for here to clear ice. Frodsham Weir on the Weaver Navigation during the 'Great Frost' of 1895.

NEW BUILDING
AND OLD

62 Montgomeryshire Canal (a part of the Shropshire Union network), Eastern Branch. Berriew Aqueduct about 1895 being repuddled due to fissuring of the bottom. Originally such work was carried out by driving cattle back and forth, here men with big boots are used.

63 When steam tugs were first introduced on the Grand Junction Canal the tunnels rapidly became clogged with soot. When this brush was first used in Blisworth Tunnel in the 1870s 10 tons of soot were shifted. The men leaned on the remote ends of the brush arms to make the necessary contact with walls and roof.

64 *Right* Blisworth Tunnel, Grand Junction Canal. Occasionally – thankfully rarely – it is necessary to renew the brickwork in a tunnel. The method of working is unchanged except for the provision of a (smelly) petrol or diesel pump in lieu of a man with a moustache.

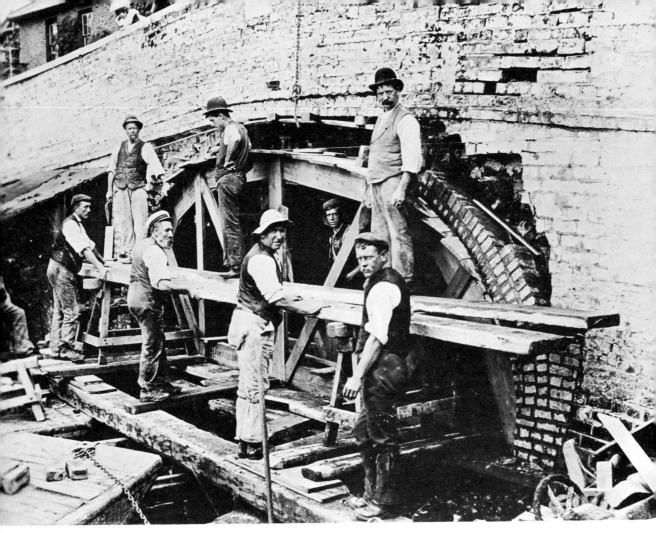

65 Hunton Bridge, between Watford & Kings Langley, Grand Junction Canal, *c.* 1900. When the arch collapsed the canal was closed for only two days; the method of 'centering' – used both as a support and to ensure correct profile – would be unchanged if this bridge collapsed tomorrow.

66 *Left* River Thames, the iron girders are for a new railway line feeding the gasworks at St Ebbe's, Oxford. Photographed in the late 1880s, somewhat unusually cabin rather than open boats have been impressed for use.

67　*Top* Hey ho and up she rises. The positioning of three girders, each weighing 9 tons, was completed on the 4th of May 1905. Wedlake Street Foot Bridge, Harrow Road, Paddington.

68　*Above* Bridging a navigation: building the Hull and Barnsley Railway, *c.* 1884.

69 A mystery photograph, possibly on the Thames and Severn Canal. Photographs of a barrow-run and a horse-jenny are extremely rare.

70 Monday the 12th of April 1909. Cleaning mud from Paddington basin. The roses and castles on Henry Boyer's boat show the pride of the captain. Note that we have, as today, three workers and seven watchers.

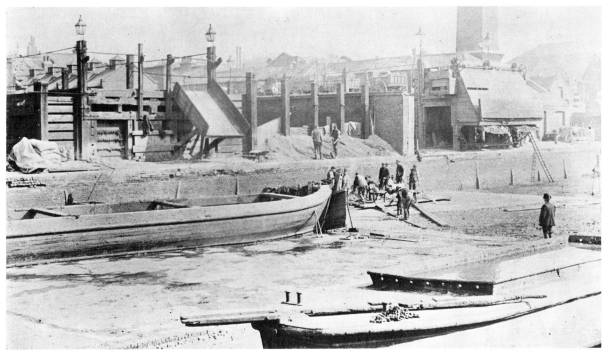

71 Paddington Basin after de-watering, 12th of April 1909. Interestingly the types of boat – a 'butty' or unpowered boat, and a mud-hopper (foreground) – are identical to those in use today for similar work. The gaslamps indicate the state of trade, with all-night loading, at the time.

72 No. 16 South Wharf, Paddington Basin. The job complete the workmen, ganger (second from left) and the superintendent (right) pose for their audience.

73 and **74**   Foxton inclined plane on the (Old) Grand Union Canal; 307 feet long it gave a rise of 75 feet. Opened in 1900, it was closed shortly after as the irregular craft movements made the steam-fired machinery uneconomic; the already extant flight of locks was restored to use.

75 Anderton Lift providing a communication between the River Weaver and the Trent & Mersey Canal. Designed by Sir E. Leader Williams (see no. 16) and opened in 1875 it is shown here more or less as built. It was subsequently converted from interconnected hydraulic siphons – the two narrow boat lifts counterbalancing one another – to independent electrical operation.

76 Taken about 1882, the photograph shows the port of Morwellham with the Tavistock Canal's inclined plane (right, middle distance) running up the hill almost parallel with railway incline. The sailing ship is lying in the Tamar Manure Canal.

77 *Left, above* Repuddling of canal bottom. The batter or slope of the sides of the waterway is apparent.

78 *Left* A bottom-end gate on the Grand Junction Canal. The gate is being raised by means of a sheer-legs, the use of a paddle-hole to take the chain is rather unusual. It consistently appears in these photographs that the workmen were elderly.

79 *Above* Lock reconstruction. This has to be posed, no canal ever had that many men available at once! Bowlers were worn as safety helmets.

80 Navigation Lock, Mildenhall, during the works on the River Lark 1909.

ON LOCATION

81 The building of the Manchester Ship Canal. Piling in progress using a 'Long Tom' hammer.

82 The lock gates on the Manchester Ship Canal were built *in situ*; seen here is Eastham 1892.

83 Manchester Ship Canal, Eastham Locks, immediately prior to their opening for traffic, 1st January 1894.

84 The chain mechanism for opening gates is clearly depicted in this photograph of Eastham Lock, Manchester Ship Canal.

85 Hartford Locks – removed 1891 – on the River Weaver. The boat is an oddity inasmuch as it has no cabin, but seemingly a 'family' crew. The tall river towing mast differs radically from that of an orthodox narrow boat.

86 Long Buckby, Grand Junction Canal, a turn of the century équipage. Three brothers – two magnificent boats. The 'Turks' Heads' on the tillers are unusually elaborate.

87 The pride of a boatman. A steamer and her butty with all the traditional equipment. Note the horse's tail as in no. 23.

88 *Above* Under the Railway & Canal Traffic Act, 1888, when upon the application of a local authority or three or more landowners adjoining or near a canal, it appeared to the Board of Trade that the canal, or part of it, had for at least three years been disused or unfit for navigation, the Board of Trade had power to authorize its abandonment. Here Captain Harmsworth is attempting to get his boat *Basingstoke*, laden with 10 tons of sand, through the Basingstoke Canal in 1913 at Mapledurwell Bridge, following a threat of closure.

89 *Left* Chelmer & Blackwater Navigation, Beeleigh, *c.* 1900. Empty timber barge returning home.

90 *Right* Superb architecture, placid waters. The coal for this power station seen in the 1890s was brought by barge.

91 Grand Junction Canal, Blisworth Tunnel, around 1900. The 'hovel' for leggers is on the left-hand side together with the horse path.

92 *Below* River Thames, Osney Lock and Mill, 1865.

93   Thames & Severn Canal: lock and odd round lockhouse at Lechlade, near the junction with the
River Thames, about 1912.

94   Thames & Severn Canal: Sapperton Tunnel at Daneway, *c.* 1905.

95 *Left* Somerset Coal Canal weigh-dock, used for gauging or weighing boats at Midford.

96 *Left, below* Glamorganshire Canal, Cardiff. North Road, Lock No. 49. The horizontal paddle gearing was rare.

97 *Below* After the thaw, Dartford Creek, 1895.

98 *Top* A slight mishap to the *Orange*. A piece of oakum was dislodged and down she went.

99 A boat belonging to Westleys, the millowners of Northampton. 'Full bags were put on top of empties, she got a blow [wind] on her long side, and over she went!'

100 After capsizing in Brentford Dock the *Stockport* was raised on Friday, 27th May 1910. It did not improve Madam Boatlady's china – or language!

101 The largest boat to reach Worcester, transhipping 170 tons of cargo into Severn & Canal Carrying Company's narrowboats, 28th September 1895.

102 Trade was booming in this photograph of Ellesmere Port, Shropshire Union Canal, 1900.

103 Braunston. A canal gathering just prior to the Great War.

105 Kennet & Avon Canal. Twenty-Nine Locks to Heaven at Devizes.

106 *Bottom* River Weaver, Dutton Locks, 1884. Dutton viaduct at rear.

107 *Right* A pair of boats working down Foxton Locks (Old) Grand Union Canal on a wet and murky day.

108 *Top* Glamorganshire Canal, Cardiff. The rather clumsy boat makes a contrast with those on the Grand Junction Canal.

109 Willow Cottage, Dartford Creek. The lock of the Dartford & Crayford Navigation is being built but the creek is still tidal; about 1900.

110 *Top* Stroudwater Canal, Eastington. Both a trow and a narrow boat are visible; the use of donkeys
on this waterway was normal.

111 Monmouthshire Canal, Pontnewydd; *c.* 1901.

112 *Right* Grand Junction Canal boats hung up at Cassio Bridge *c.* 1910.

113 *Below* Although the couple on *Shamrock* look well pleased with themselves in February 1905, they had already been frozen in for some time at Walk Mill Bridge, Chadderton on the Rochdale Canal.

114 *Top* The driver of the traction engine died in this accident at Fornham, Suffolk, on the 16th of June 1890. The navigation was closed for a few days.

115 Stratford-on-Avon Canal lifting bridge viewed from Drawbridge Farm Drive. Although extremely rustic in appearance this efficient pattern of bridge remained in use until relatively recently. It makes a contrast with the bridge on the Ellesmere Canal.

116   A congregation waits for the Rev. W. Ward of the Incorporated and Boatmen's Friend Society at Sheffield, 1909. There were a number of these societies, although this was the most realistic, running hostels (billiards, tea, buns and a prayer) and more important, stables. The Salvation Army (Brigadier and Mrs Fielding) still carry on such 'missionary' work today, using their cruiser *Pilgrim*.

117   *Right, above* Grand Junction Canal, Batchworth Lock, near Rickmansworth. An interesting geometrical study: the rather strange balance beams add to the effect.

118   *Right* The Eastern Counties Navigation & Transport Company's directors, workmen and lighter crews, pose on reaching Bury St Edmunds, September 1894, River Lark.

119 *Below* The Thames at Teddington, 1899. Nine boats are visible. The boat rollers were provided for the use of skiffs, rowboats, etc., to save water.

120 *Right* The patriachal gentleman probably knew the Bude Canal in its heyday.

121 *Right, below* Debdale Bridge and Lock No. 9, Staffs & Worcs Canal, 1890. The grey horse is unusual, since quite a number of boatmen regarded this colouring as unlucky. The attractive footbridge at the tail of the lock is a pleasant example of the ironfounder's art.

The New Docks, S.G.   J.R.

122 *Left* The New Dock, Manchester Ship Canal. Aside from the railway owned narrow boat, middle foreground, in the right-hand corner is a Leeds & Liverpool barge, while a Rochdale Canal Company's barge shows only its stern. The dredger would be useful almost anywhere today!

123 *Left, below* Empty boats right, loaded left. When the boats were empty washing was often hidden by the top-cloths. A boatshaft served well as a clothes-pole.

124 *Below* Environs of Birmingham. The canal is both wide and deep – dredging having recently taken place at the junction. The iron bridge (left) has that pleasantly unassuming 'canal look', while away in the distance a loaded boat makes its way.

125 Stoke Bruerne, Grand Junction Canal, before the war. The mill is now occupied by the Waterways Museum while the arm which went off to the right under the accommodation bridge is filled in.

Stoke Bruerne.

126　Tetney Lock on the Louth Navigation, Lincolnshire, about 1900.

TETNEY LOCK.

127 The tranquillity of this scene is almost unbelievable to us. Thames, Caversham Lock.

PLEASURE

128   Fishermen at Horning, River Brue, ignore and are ignored by passing wherries (1902).

129   Frimley Green Top Lock, Basingstoke Canal, 1906.

5 4914 Frimley Green. The Lock.

130 Drawbridge on the Ellesmere Canal, Whitchurch. The original caption reads 'My time has been very pleasantly filled in here'. Not only a charming spot, but the girl is dressed beautifully too. Note the photographer's modest talent in superimposing the figures.

131 S.S. *Gondolier* transhipping passengers to the hotel coach at Inverness, Caledonian Canal, 1904.

132 Dereliction at Stratford,
Upper Avon Navigation.

133 In their spare time Bushell Bros of Tring, Grand Junction Canal, hired out a motorized dinghy.
The dog's expression is inscrutable.

134   The lazy way through Boulters on the Thames.

54082. Maidenhead; Boulters Lock Bridge.

135   Male chauvinism at Boulters. Disgustingly the men are doing the punting while the ladies rest.

136 Great Marlow on the Thames, 1890. The clothing looks unbelievable: pity the poor washerwoman.

137 A strong wind was blowing when Payne-Jennings took this photograph of The Pleasure Boat Inn, Hickling Broad in 1879. Presumably the timber-laden wherry wasn't among the 'Boats to let'.

Arthur Beech,

Lock House, Compton,

Wolverhampton.

The Steamers 'Compton Queen,' 'Margaret,' and 'Victoria,' make sailings from Newbridge as follows :—

Monday, Coven & Calf Heath, 3 o'clock

Thursday, Brewood,   3 o'clock

Saturday, Coven or Brewood, 3 o'clock

Sunday,   Coven,   3-30 o'clock

ALL RETURN AT DUSK.

Fares, **1/-** each ; Children, **6d.** each.

Extra Trips at Holiday times.

Motor Boat runs daily throughout the season.

A fine fleet of Rowing Boats for hire, by the hour, day, or for the season.

56

138   The *Compton Queen* and her schedule.

139 The lock-keeper at Molesey Lock, River Thames, was no doubt selling flowers to the ladies and their swains in 1892.

140 Teddesley Bridge, Staffs & Worcs Canal. The ornamental work (on the bridge, not the girls!) was insisted upon by the local landowner as part of the price to be paid for cutting through his land.

141 Sunday school outing on Harry King's boats, Grand Junction Canal, about 1910. There were about 200 children and adults on board.

142 *Above* Warmsworth on the navigable river Dun (Sheffield & South Yorkshire Navigation) *c.* 1870. Children never can stand still!

143 *Right* Thames, Sonning Lock. The horse-drawn houseboat was a common sight.

SPRING LOCK, BERKSHIRE. 7958. G.W.W.

144 *Left* Replete after their breakfast (eggs, bacon, kidneys, etc.) the three men on a Fen's boat wash up prior to an amble up the River Yare.

145 *Left, below* In direct contrast with the skiffs and punts of the Thames, both the Ouse and Humber had a number of these paddlers, which plied their watery wastes (although the banks are still visible) both as ferries and trip-boats. Meks a change from t'mill! Around 1900.

146 *Below* Sunday School outing on the Brecon & Abergavenny Canal at Gilwern, *c.* 1890.

147 Sunbury Lock, River Thames. The steam tug and her consort are working upstream with a load of (probably) potatoes. There is no doubt, however, that the girl is a tempting target!

THE REASON WHY

148 Canal traffic magnificat! The cotton shed on the Manchester Ship Canal, 1890. Brought largely by the Leeds & Liverpool and Rochdale Canals, this cotton also includes surats from India awaiting on-carriage.

149 River Welland, Spalding Gas Works. The quay is being reconstructed for use by coal-carrying Humber keels, 1900.

150 Fellows, Morton & Clayton pair awaiting transhipment at Fazeley Street Wharves, Birmingham. The photograph neatly shows the latest forms of transport, the Bollinder-engined *Lapwing* and the steam waggon, *c.* 1910.

151 *Below* Hayfield Road Wharf, Oxford Canal, *c.* 1895. The boat people are dressed to show off: the boats, wharf, coal, carts and the maid all belong to Frank Restall.

152 River Thames at Marlow Suspension Bridge. Loading round timber, 1900. The use of screw jacks enables the ganger (middle, smoking pipe) to have a natter! Incidentally, how did the man on the left manage to smoke a clay pipe while doing such work?

153 *Top* Once famed for its delicate and beautiful work, the Nantgarw Pottery had already fallen on hard times when this photograph was taken around 1890. Glamorganshire Canal.

154 Derby Canal, Little Eaton Gangway, closed 1908. Container traffic is not new – the boxes transhipped from tram-carriage to boat are just discernible and first came into use in 1795.

155 *Left* Honeystreet Wharf on the Kennet and Avon Canal around 1905. Although this was a railway-owned canal nevertheless the towpath appears well maintained and the canal clear of weed.

156 *Left, below* Somerset people, probably on the navigable drains of Sedgemoor, 1904. The cargo is peat, used both as a fertilizer and as a fuel.

157 *Below* Where once feet trod. Packet House, Worsley, Bridgewater Canal, 1880, used originally by passengers embarking and disembarking on the Duke of Bridgewater's pleasure craft.

158 By the 10th of May 1911 the brickworks at Braunston had become a mud tip, used for the disposal of dredging waste.

OUSE TRANSPORT Co.,

CARRIERS BY WATER BETWEEN

LYNN, ST. IVES, HUNTINGDON, ST. NEOTS, BEDFORD,

AND INTERMEDIATE PLACES ON THE

OUSE NAVIGATION-

SEE PLAN ON BACK.

SEE PLAN ON B.

For Rates and other Information APPLY TO

Chief Offices: Duck Mill Lane, BEDFORD.   *W. THORNBER, Manager.*

Lynn Office: St. Ann's Fort, KING'S LYNN.   *W. S. ALLEN, Agent.*

Huntingdon Office: } Navigation Yard, GODMANCHESTER.   *J. BULL, Agent.*

THROUGH RATES QUOTED TO OR FROM

Glasgow, Grangemouth, Edinburgh, Newcastle, Hull, Hamburg, Rouen, &c.

BY ARRANGEMENT WITH THE

Carron, East Coast, Lynn & Hamburg, and Lynn & Rouen Steamship Co's.

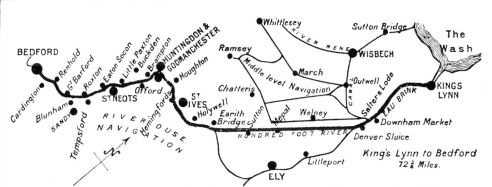

VARIOUS GOODS RECENTLY CARRIED ON OUSE NAVIGATION.

Wheat, Barley, Oats, Maize, Bran, Flour, Beans, Offals.
Timber, Deals, Boards, Firewood, Laths, Wood Paving Blocks, Furniture, &c.
Pig Iron, Castings, Fire Grates and Ranges, Lamp Posts, Rain Water Pipes, Guttering, Nails, Machinery, &c.
Coals, Granite, Moulding Sand, Brick Silt, Gas Tar, Gas Water, Petroleum, Whiting, &c.
Sugar, Soda, Soap, Starch, Rice, Washing Powders, Candles, Oranges, Onions, Lemons, Earthenware, &c.
Drain Pipes, Slates, Hair, Cement, Tiles, Chimney Pots, Ridges, and other Builders' Sundries, &c.
Compressed Straw and Hay, Peat Moss, Mangolds, Carrots, Linseed Cake, &c.
Rags, Wood Pulp, Sackings, Jute, Yarns, &c.   *Bedford, December, 1895,*

161　Clearing a road on the Birmingham Canal Navigations, Main Line, *c.* 1900. Ice-breaker left-hand side of canal in the distance, gongoozlers left-hand towpath.

162　Grand Junction Canal, Rickmansworth; the contrast between the pair of narrow boats and the hay-laden barge is rather impressive.

163 This area is now buried under Nuffield College. Oxford Canal, turn of the century. The stack is of 'black diamonds' – coal.

164 *Below* The battery of fenders on the bows of Albert Wood's boat *Bedford*, seen here at Castleton, Rochdale Canal, all serve a purpose: top and middle for 'stemming' (bashing) open gates, the bottom for protection against the lock-cill.

165 *Right* Sheffield & South Yorkshire Navigation (River Dun Navigation), Conisbrough c. 1908. Load: round timber. One horse, 50–60 tons.

166 *Left* Lincoln, Cornmill Wharf on the River Witham, about 1900.

167 Keadby, River Trent, junction with Stainforth & Keadby Canal, around 1890. Coal loading wharves and windmill typify the era.

168 The end and the beginning. Liverpool Docks about 1895–1900; the boats on the left may well have been on their way via the Leeds & Liverpool Canal to Wigan Pier. Cotton ('poor man's silk') in, coal ('black diamonds') out. And so the circle is completed.